# God and President Trump plus the Rest of Us

PATRIC RUTHERFORD PHD

God and President Trump plus the Rest of Us
Copyright 2017 Patric Rutherford PHD
All rights reserved.

ISBN 10: 0692855416
ISBN 13: 9780692855416

Library of Congress Control Number: 2017903290
Patric R. Rutherford, Apopka, FL

All scripture quotations taken from the Holy Bible, New International Version (NIV). Copyright 1973, 1978, 1984, and 2011 by Biblica, Inc. Used with permission. All rights reserved worldwide.

# DISCLAIMER

The author of this book is not a mental-health professional, and nothing in it is to be used as a prescription for the treatment of mental illness or as a substitute for consulting with a mental-health professional.

# DEDICATION

*I dedicate this book to the memory of my parents, Lucille and William. To my mother, who gave me the blocks for character formation, and my father, whose memories bring me thoughts of forgiveness and divine transformation.*

# ACKNOWLEDGMENTS

We all need friends who will keep us honest and true to our better selves. At the top of my list is Ruth, my darling wife, who has been a great support to me through the years and whose keen eyes have helped me determine what to keep and what to throw in the writing of this book. I am able to write this material today because of those who have been my teachers and those who have had a positive influence on my life—to them I will remain eternally grateful.

Most of all, I thank God, who inspired me to write and sustained me in the process.

# TABLE OF CONTENTS

1. Introduction — 1
2. President Trump — 3
3. The Responsibility of the Presidency — 9
4. God — 15
5. The Mental Health of the Nation — 21
6. Haters of President Trump — 27
7. Those Who Love President Trump — 33
8. Importance of Truth — 37
9. Lessons from Rulers Past — 43
10. Moses — 45
11. Saul and David — 49
12. Solomon and Rehoboam—a Kingdom Divided — 53
13. Ahaz and Isaiah—Faith in Man or God — 57
14. Nebuchadnezzar and Cyrus — 59
15. Mahatma Gandhi (1869–1948) — 65
16. Adolf Hitler (1889–1945) — 69
17. Nelson Mandela (1918–2013) — 75
18. The Challenge for Christian Leadership in Today's World — 81
19. Jesus Christ as a Leader — 85
20. The Path Forward — 91
21. Conclusion — 97

# INTRODUCTION

To say life is complex is to state the obvious, and there are few places where it gets more complex than at the intersection of church and state, religion and politics, and spirituality and governance.

In religion we enter the world of metaphysics (life beyond physics), where we seek to answer the questions of the purpose and meaning of life and life after death. In the world of government, we deal with law and order, economic growth and development, and public safety and infrastructure for communications and transportation.

The meeting of these two rivers of the human experience flushes to the surface our souls' highest hopes and our deepest fears. When the pillar of either structure is shaken, we are most troubled in our spirits, and uncertainty becomes the order of the day.

When the systems of government are in upheaval, those who are spiritual usually find in their spiritual lives an anchor that holds them, a source of strength, inspiration for hope, and a reference point from which to cast a new positive vision for the future.

It is our spirituality that shapes our philosophies of life and that determines how we govern. From the wellspring of our souls where they connect with the divine, we draw the spiritual water needed to form our codes of ethics, build character, and structure the kind of governance system that best serves the greater good of all.

When our spiritual lives are shaken and we lose the divine perspective, we are prone to look more to government to meet our needs and secure our future; at this precarious place, we make our political leaders our gods, giving them adulation and homage no human should give to another and developing expectations of them far beyond their capacity to deliver.

This scenario sets us up for deep disappointment when our leaders fail to deliver what they promised or what we expected, and if we are unwilling to accept their humanness and consequent capacity to fail, our minds migrate to a delusional world where we make believe that our leaders should remain on the pedestals we have placed them and blame others for their failure.

Amid the uncertainties of these times, the strivings of the many forces that shape our sociopolitical world, we need a guiding light. History and revelation have shown that God is our only safe guide into the future. This book seeks to present that perspective.

# PRESIDENT TRUMP

On November 8, 2016, the United States of America voted to elect Donald Trump to be its next president. Now that the election is over, some Christians may be asking the question, how did a man seemingly so unlike Christ become president of the United States, which is supposed to be a Christian country? Then we have to remind ourselves that the United States is not officially a Christian country—the founding fathers ensured in the writing of the Constitution and the setting up of the structure of the government that there was a clear separation of church and state.

So while 70 percent of the country is Christian, the government is structured to be secular, and there is no mandate that whoever is elected president has to be Christian in name or practice. While my value system, based on my God-respecting belief and heritage, may find some things unacceptable in a leader, I must respect the right of others to choose whom they wish without trying to impose my value system on their decision-making.

In elections we are rarely faced with a choice between someone who completely shares our values and someone else who does not. Most times there are gray areas, and there are times when we are faced with choices that are less than ideal, and most of us struggle with choosing the lesser of two evils.

Even with that perspective, I am still surprised at the outcome of the election. The harsh language used in mocking and putting down his opponents in the primaries, the statements that showed gross insensitivity and disrespect to the feelings of persons of various sectors of the electorate, his gross disregard for the truth, and his rude utterances about elected leaders within his own party made me think he was unelectable. To make sense of it, I ask why people vote for someone to be president of this country, and I hear this voice in my head saying, "It's the economy; have you forgotten?"

I have long been convinced that in a general election most people vote their economic interests and not necessarily the values expounded by their faith. And once the decision is made regarding whom they plan to vote for, like young lovers, they become so deliriously infatuated with the candidate that their eyes are blind to the glaring moral flaws of the person, which could spell problems for the country in the future.

No doubt this is one of the most unusual of candidates to run for president of the United States. He is a man of means who is used to speaking his mind and likes making extreme statements without regard in most instances to how others, who may be offended, feel about what he says, or who knowingly says extreme things (sometimes extremely untruthful things) to create a certain effect.

This is so very unlike the value system taught in the Christian faith. The values of the Christian faith emanate from our belief in God as creator and our acceptance of his call to love him supremely and to love our neighbors as ourselves. This leads to respect for others, which causes us to treat them with kindness and dignity as exemplified in the story of the Good Samaritan. A relationship with God leads us to a life of humility, which is the opposite of arrogance, boastfulness, and vanity.

President Trump must be credited for recognizing the gross discontent the public had for the Washington establishment and the crying need of Middle America, which has been left behind despite recent strides in the growth of the US economy. He spoke to their need, and they responded with their votes.

Having won the election, can he now deliver on the promises he made to them? The question is not whether he *wants* to but whether he *can*.

He has two great challenges to making that delivery. One is the reason for the loss of jobs in the first place. The losses were caused by three major forces. One is the technological revolution, which allows manufacturers to produce more goods with less manpower.

Second is globalization, which has opened the door for manufacturers to produce their goods in other countries where labor cost is much lower and at the same quality standard in most instances as in the United States.

And third, those who invest in production that creates jobs do so because they want to make a profit and are attracted to countries where operating cost and taxes are lower. Their missions are to make a profit and not necessarily to grow the US economy or generate jobs for Americans.

The second challenge President Trump faces is himself. He has been a part of the system that is focused on making more and more money, getting richer and richer. That mind-set is not what it takes to do something special for out-of-work or underemployed Americans. To deliver what he promised requires a change of heart, what we in the Christian faith call conversion, and for that he needs God.

We hope that in going to Washington to drain the swamp, he does not become the alligator in chief.

People do not change easily. They may modify their behavior to suit a situation, but until they decide to change and put focus and energy to it, they remain the same. They are usually stimulated to change when they have an aha moment, a point in time when they become aware that there is a need to embrace a new direction for their lives because the old way of doing things is not taking them where they need to go, or an eye-opening experience that shoves in their faces the consciousness of the pain they are causing themselves or others.

God is available to him and is eager to help him solve the nation's problems, because God loves and cares for Middle America and all Americans far more than President Trump does. The question is, is he willing to look to God for help?

Clearly President Trump is not a leader of God's church and is not expected to pursue an ecclesiastical role on behalf of the affairs of the church or have as his main agenda the church's mission for society. But his actions do affect people, all of whom are God's creatures, loved and cared for by him. As his actions affect people, they interface with God's plan for them and the direction he is taking the world. Though the paths seem divergent, they do intersect in significant ways in the unfolding history of our world.

Is there some great good deep within President Trump's soul that God in his great plan will bring out in due time to transform society into something more beautiful and functional for the greater good of all? Is he to accomplish such great things that are now hidden from the view of the pessimistic onlooker that will cause him or her to gasp with amazement when they finally unfold?

Or is God planning to use him as he did Nebuchadnezzar and Cyrus for some special purpose in his plan for the world? Or will he be like a Lyndon Johnson, who created havoc with the Vietnam War but also upgraded the Social Security system to include Medicare and Medicaid, which is of benefit to millions of Americans today?

Maybe God has allowed Donald Trump to win so that Americans can face the reality of their rejection of him and their worship of their new gods: money, entertainment, and celebrities.

The opportunity is there for President Trump to do exceptionally well and make a significant difference in the progress of our country and our world. God is always ready to work with him and each of us if we are willing to let him into our hearts.

# THE RESPONSIBILITY OF THE PRESIDENCY

Based on the election rhetoric, for some the task before President Trump is fixing the economy, especially for those who feel left behind; solving the illegal immigration problem; and coming up with a better health-care plan than that which is provided for in the Affordable Care Act (Obamacare). The role and responsibilities of the president go way beyond that.

According to the Declaration of Independence, the role of the US government is to secure the rights of its citizens to "Life, Liberty, and the pursuit of Happiness." The president is responsible for providing leadership to this end.

The best leader is the one who leads by example. The preservation of life and liberty goes beyond the effective policing and maintenance of a functional judiciary. It involves engendering in the citizenry a deep and mutual respect for each other, with respect to both life and property.

The teaching of respect for others by leaders is best done by modeling.

It is therefore the responsibility of the president, all elected officials, and the rest of us who have leadership roles in society to model respect for others. For some this does not come easy. To respect others we must first respect ourselves. We cannot give to another that which we do not have for ourselves.

The source of self-respect is also mentioned in the Declaration of Independence: "That all men are created equal, that they are endowed by their Creator with certain unalienable Rights." When we see ourselves as children of God, created by him equal to all others and at the same time unique, loved, and cared for by the creator, placed here by him for a purposeful life, we value ourselves.

When we see value in ourselves, we have self-respect, and as we recognize the same value God has placed on others, we come to value them and respect them too. If we disrespect others, we also show disrespect for God, their creator.

The Declaration of Independence also speaks to the "pursuit of Happiness." Happiness is found in relationships. You can have all the wealth you dream of in the world, but if you do not have someone to share your life with, you are only a rich, lonely, unhappy soul. Money cannot buy happiness. It only facilitates our being able to create an environment of sharing so that we can have the joy of blessing others with our lives.

Good relationships are based on trust. The people we are closest to are the people we trust with our feelings. When we disrespect the people around us, we break trust and destroy relationships. In doing so we create emotional pain for others and guilt and remorse for ourselves—there is no happiness in that.

Trust is built on evidence. By being loving, honest, and truthful, we show our trustworthiness. Relationships that are not built on trust are usually dysfunctional, involving people who are codependents or people using each other to get what they want without contributing anything to anyone's happiness.

True nation building involves the building of relationships between peoples in a spirit of mutual respect. The president has a pivotal role in providing leadership in this direction. He needs to model integrity to the nation. Like the rest of us, he has to learn to forgive past hurts and forge ahead, seeking peace for the nation in its internal and external relationships.

We saw the outpouring of love and support that was shown in this country after 9/11. It was a demonstration of what we are capable of if we are willing to put our hearts and minds to it. It should not take another disaster of that magnitude to unite us for the common good—visionary leadership and the blessings of God can take us there.

The rising tide does not raise all boats because some boats are too damaged, sitting on a sand bar, so it will only sink them, drowning their occupants. It is the responsibility of the government led by the president to find a way for all, or most, Americans to have a piece of the pie—as challenging as that may be.

We must not lose sight of the fact that money without morals is a prescription for the deterioration of a nation. While morality cannot be legislated, if we are to become a better people, integrity must be modeled, especially by those in leadership positions. The president is at the top of the pile, and he needs to give our children something to aspire to.

Money will not take hate from our hearts or fear from our souls. The time will come when the darkness of our humanness will visit us with grief, overshadowing our joys and triumphs with sorrow and hopelessness—those times when deep calls to deep and our own thoughts cave in on us. In those times we need a force greater than our humanness can muster or money can buy. We need God and those he would use to minister to our souls.

If we sacrifice servility and kindness in our quest to get economic growth, when the money comes to us, we will use it to hurt each other because we act out what is in our hearts. Prosperity does not always bring peace. Peace of mind and joy of heart are not dependent on financial prosperity.

While having what is needed to take care of our family is important, who we become in the process is more important. We can have stuff and become such hateful, unhappy persons that the same family we are providing for does not want to live with us.

# GOD AND PRESIDENT TRUMP PLUS THE REST OF US

To be successful, President Trump needs to be the "uniter in chief." Unity enhances the ability of the nation to focus its energies collaboratively in a positive direction. Far more is accomplished in a team effort than from individual work. An individual may invent something great, but it takes a team to build it and successfully market it.

Unity is not affected by the mentality of "Get under my umbrella, or I will crush you" but by openness, mutual respect, the creation of a trusting environment, and the pursuit of common goals.

Leaders who believe they know it all often conclude it's their role to think for everybody else. They determine in their minds what is best for society and seek to force others to conform to their way of thinking.

This is accomplished by trying to make detractors think they are not bright if they do not share the leader's opinion, or give the impression that those in disagreement with them are not acting in the national interest, and when that fails, leaders resort to the creation of fear. If you are afraid of someone, it is your fear that gives power to that person over you.

Another role of the president is "comforter in chief." In times of natural disasters and great personal loss that affect the nation, its citizens look to their leader for comfort. To be good at comforting requires compassion. When the chips are down and the pain and suffering of one sector bleed across to the rest of the nation, we should be able to look to the president for the attitude and words that will lift us beyond partisan divides, denominational differences, and ethnic and social barriers to stand by each other in consolation and for the moving of our souls for the greater good.

To do the best job possible, President Donald Trump needs God, as well as his wisdom, knowledge, and understanding.

# GOD

God is the creator of the universe, and that means he cannot be defined by what exists in our universe. A full picture of who God is is beyond us. However, we can conceptualize a limited image of him. As creator he is not limited by time and location because he created time and space. We can imagine him looking at the universe and our world as you would view a video game in which you can see all the moves that have been made up to the present. With perfect knowledge of the rules of the game and the back-end software that controls it, you can see all the possible outcomes of all the possible moves before you.

With that level of knowledge and control of the game, you can make the right moves (choices) to ensure the game ends the way you want it to.

Similarly, God is viewing our world with a panoramic view of our past and perfect knowledge of everything happening at present and of all the possible outcomes of our choices in the future. He is seeing everything at a glance.

He is dealing with all the possibilities of all the outcomes of all our possible choices—how our decisions will affect others, their reactions, and the chain reaction from that into the future.

God has given us the power of choice because he wants to interact with us at a relational level. If we did not have the power of choice, we would be robots, programmed to do exactly what he wants. He would find that boring. God is a god of love and has created us with the capacity to respond to him as intelligent beings choosing on our own volition to love him in return or live selfishly.

Since he has given us the power of choice, he has not fixed the future. Our future is the result of our choices, natural and supernatural forces at play in our world, and his interventions in guiding the world toward his desired end in accordance with his divine purpose.

While God loves us and respects our power of choice, he will not allow us to choose to eradicate knowledge of him from the world. Those who have tried have succeeded at times in making the lives of believers turbulent but in the end have found their efforts were futile. Ultimately no one can win a fight against God.

As we look at our history, we see the many times God has had to intervene in human affairs to prevent us from destroying each other and the world.

God is not only intent on preserving knowledge of himself in our world—he is filling it with the light of his presence, constantly calling and empowering humans to rise above their baser selves and the tyranny of others to a place of love, joy, and meaningfulness. One day the game as it is played now will end, evil will be totally removed, and love will reign forever.

For many God is relegated to times of disaster—the graveside, the sickbed, the moments in our lives when we desperately need something our money cannot buy and our influence cannot produce, those moments when life tumbles in and the darkness of hopelessness covers our land. He is available for us at those times, but he also wants to make the other times of our lives beautiful with his presence.

God wants us to recognize him as our god and to choose to worship and honor him as such. When we put God first, the principles of his kingdom become our principles. We love others as he loves us. When we do good for the pure joy of blessing others, we are being like God in our world, but when we do good with selfish motives so we can be seen and praised by others, then we have made idols of ourselves, and our worship is self-worship.

After the bombing of the World Trade Center, New Yorkers flocked to churches in large numbers, but as soon as they got past the fear and the grief, for many, things returned to business as usual.

While church attendance is a significant force in upholding the name of God in the world, church is not the only place God shows himself. He is god of the universe and is involved in all the affairs of our world. He is behind every movement to remove pain and suffering, free the oppressed, bring peace and joy to human hearts, and spread love in the world.

God's love is extended to all. In every country and every culture, he is present, making the crops grow so people have food to eat and filling parents' hearts with love for their children, so they are nurtured and cared for until they can stand on their own. When there is famine, war, and natural disasters, he moves the hearts of those who are willing and able to go to the rescue of those in need.

God wants to be more than a fireman to us or a tool that we reach for when we want to get something done. He is available for far more than getting us out of trouble when we have a problem we can't fix ourselves. He wants a relationship with each one of us through which he can bless our lives from within, bringing us the transformation we need to be truly loving people who relate well to those around us.

Good relationships are not built on occasional acts of kindness but on consistency in kindness, truthfulness, and love. God wants us to become like him and show his goodness to the world. There is a lot of good in the world, but goodness is always in danger when selfishness and dishonesty rise.

When we talk about God, some people's minds come to focus on religion, and if they have had a negative experience with religion, they have difficulty reaching out to God. God transcends religion. Religion is like a means of transportation, not a destination. Fellowship with God, fellow believers, and a life of service is what we are called to. Religion facilitates our getting there.

When a religion becomes an end in itself, so cold and unchangeable that God's character cannot be seen in it, it is time to do something to change it or find a new vehicle. When a life is surrendered to God, he will lead that soul to a faith community that will enhance his or her spiritual growth and lead that person into a life of service.

As God executes his plan for the future of our world, each of us, from president to illegal immigrant, has a choice as to how we align with earth's unfolding history. We have a choice between love and hate, good and evil, and truth and falsehood.

God is sovereign and is intimately involved in every aspect of our lives and every activity in our world. Life is therefore not a game we play in which we make our own rules as we go along. God has set the rules—he is the ultimate moral authority, and all are accountable to him.

If we choose to allow him into our lives, he will give us the power to live lives of love and integrity filled with joy and purpose.

# THE MENTAL HEALTH OF THE NATION

A national election is a time of high emotions. People on opposite sides say and do things to each other that create emotional pain and strain relationships. Then there is the letdown for those whose party did not win and the sometimes euphoric elation of those whose side won. We often do not take into account the impact of all the negatives on the population and the need for postelection healing and recovery.

During the election campaign, several comments were made on national television about Mr. Trump's mental health, specifically claiming that he suffers from narcissistic personality disorder. Before we start throwing stones at him on this matter, let's take a look at the matter of mental health from a broader perspective.

One day some men took a woman to Jesus whom they had caught in the act of adultery. (I wonder whether they caught the man.) They told him that according to the Law of Moses she should be stoned and asked him for his judgment. It was a neat trap. If he said she should be stoned, he would be going against Roman law, which only allowed Roman officials to order executions. If he said she should go free, they would accuse him of going against the Law of Moses.

Jesus asked that the person without sin cast the first stone. One by one they left until only the woman was left with Jesus. The reality of mental-health issues in our society is one in which it is dangerous to point fingers, play games, or start throwing stones. All of us are prone to mental illness.

Those of us who appear sane today may have a problem surface tomorrow. Or it may be one of our family members, friends, or coworkers. From data compiled by the Substance Abuse and Mental Health Services Administration, it is estimated that one in five Americans suffered from mental illness in 2014. These illnesses included depression, anxiety, bipolar disorder, personality disorders, and schizophrenia, to name a few.

There are people we work with, sit beside at church, interact with on social media, or live with who have mental illness. Some we know about; most we don't. There are those who are fully functional, are receiving the appropriate care for their conditions, and pose no threat to themselves or society. Others have to be institutionalized until they are well enough to be functional in society.

There are those who are not aware of or are in denial about mental-health conditions they have while it is obvious to others around them. The challenge with mental health is that the part of our beings that tells when we are dysfunctional is the very part that is not fully functional or not functioning at all. Putting it another way, the part of us that tells us that something is wrong (our abilities to rationally assess the appropriateness of our own behaviors) is the part that is not working right.

Caring family members and friends should take seriously the responsibility to help those close to them face the awareness that their behavior is inappropriate and help them seek professional help. As a part of the illness itself, the mentally ill may not be as aware as we think they are of how out of touch they are with reality.

Fortunately for those of us who live in the United States, there is not as strong a stigma associated with mental illnesses as there is in some other parts of the world. So there is a greater willingness to acknowledge that a problem exists and seek professional help for it. As with most other illnesses, the earlier a person recognize that something is not right and seek professional help, the better the chance of full recovery.

God can and does help us with our mental-health issues. A relationship with him brings to the soul a sense of security and peace, which is essential for good mental health. For those whose mental health is already compromised, asking God for miraculous healing alone is not always the answer. He may choose to help you through the aid of a mental-health professional because most often there are underlying behavioral issues that need to be addressed that a divine pill will not fix.

For example, a man is suffering from depression that was triggered by his wife, the love of his life, leaving him for another man. He feels betrayed and becomes angry with her and hateful toward her new lover. He is worried about his economic survival because he cannot afford the house payment on his salary alone and child support at the same time. He is in a desperate spot and is trying to drown his sorrows with alcohol. He realizes he is depressed and cries out to God for relief from depression.

God answers yes, and the depression is gone. But the underlying cause for the depression was not addressed—he has not grieved the loss of his wife, let go of the anger and hatred, or quit the drinking. In a few days, he will likely be depressed again.

There is a similarity between spiritual- and mental-health restorations. Spiritual healing comes when we acknowledge that our lives are not what they ought to be, go to God, and ask for forgiveness and a restored relationship with him through the salvation he has provided in Jesus Christ. By humbly surrendering ourselves to God, we open our hearts for the infilling of his love and the opportunity for better relationships with fellow humans.

The restoration of our mental health is somewhat similar. There has to be some acknowledgment that something is not right about our thinking and a willingness to seek help to make things right. Trying to fix ourselves by ourselves with minds that are not working right does not always work.

There are times when we recognize that we are not right with our thinking or actions, and we are able to make the necessary adjustments to get ourselves back on track. Other times we try hard and pray hard, but the changes are not happening; then it's time to seek professional help.

People who relate to life out of their pain can become so consumed by anger and hate that the emotional parts of the brains hijack the reasoning parts of the brains, using it to carry out their evil devising (self-centered overprotective maneuvers and revenge).

When we allow God in our lives, he works through our reasoning to reprogram our emotions, replacing fear with faith, anger and hatred with forgiveness, and discontent with peace and joy.

Brain chemistry influences our thoughts, and our thoughts and other sensory inputs influence brain chemistry. Some mental illnesses are influenced by chemical imbalances in the brain. It takes a professional to assess that and help with the return to balance.

Whether it is restoring one's relationship with God or making things right with one's fellow man, acknowledging wrong and expressing sorrow for it is a critical component. The inability to say "I am sorry" comes from an overwhelming need to save face.

This usually results from exposure to an extremely shame-based environment that has caused the individual to have poor self-image. A person who sees himself as inherently good does not see one bad deed as defining his whole person if he should do something bad. Such an individual is much more willing to admit wrong because the wrong does not define him.

On the other hand, person who see himself as bad interpret his wrongdoing as a consequence of his nature and thus do not want to admit to it, even to himself. To admit that he has done wrong is to define his entire being as being bad. His ego, in protecting itself, recoil at that thought and won't go there.

Until the problem of self-perception is fixed, living in a self-created alternate world where one is never wrong is, for an individual, the order of the day. For the rest of us, that will at some point become unbearable.

# HATERS OF PRESIDENT TRUMP

President Trump has said some things that have created excruciating emotional pain far beyond what he may have intended or understood. This has made many people angry. If we hate him for it, we too will be functioning out of our pain and will become insensitive to the hurt we create in others.

Anger is usually the prelude to hate. Anger that is not properly processed and is allowed to settle in the mind over time becomes hate. Anger is a natural response we have when we go through an experience that makes us feel threatened, whether the threat or perceived threat is to our physical or emotional wellness.

When the brain perceives a threat, there are automatic responses that are triggered to deal with the threat in what is called the fight-or-flight response system. The person or thing that is perceived as the source of the threat is stored in memory as a possible threat for future reference. There is usually an element of fear associated with the source of the threat.

If the unfolding of the event reveals that you had no reason to fear for harm in the first place, that the party involved meant no harm or the threatening situation was so insignificant that it was not worth getting upset about, then anger subsides, and life returns to normal.

For example, if you were walking down the road and someone shouted at you to get out of the way and shoved you to the side, your initial reaction would be to become angry at this rude person invading your space, and you might even be tempted to shove back in retaliation, shouting, "How dare you touch me," only to find in a few seconds that the person had moved you out of the way of an out-of-control car that was heading straight toward you. Anger turns to gratitude.

On the other hand, if the shout and shove were expressions of hostility from a truly rude and disrespectful person, the anger would persist unless processed or unless the offending person were forgiven. Persistent anger usually turns to hate.

Like all other emotions, it will find a means of expression, both internally and externally. Thoughts affect brain chemistry, and brain chemistry affects body functions. Negative emotions such as anger produce negative thoughts, which produce changes that suppress our immune systems and can also set us up for heart attacks and strokes.

Externally, hatred causes us to lash out at the person or persons we perceive as threatening. When the animosity is aroused, the emotion can be so strong that we lose our senses of reasoning and do things we regret afterward or even go to prison for. If the object of our hatred is not present or emotional or if other ties we have with the person keep us from harming them, we may practice displaced aggression and hurt someone else.

In practicing displaced aggression, we pass on the pain of our lives to someone else, some innocent soul who does not deserve our wrath. If what we have in us is hate, what we will share with others is the pain of our lives.

Haters destroy themselves and others, often the very persons they claim to love and depend on for emotional support. Hate transforms us into people others do not want to be around.

If you hate President Trump, it's not worth it to you or to those you care for. Hate is too destructive an energy; it transforms you into the object of your hate or even worse. People who do things that are hurtful to you do what they do because of who they are, and you cannot change them.

The only person you can change is yourself, and sometimes we find it hard to change ourselves and have to cry to God for help. When there are people in our lives causing us pain, we deal with it best by adjusting our attitudes toward them by reframing how we view the situation rather than expecting them to change and become the people we expect them to be. If we are waiting for others to change, we may wait forever.

When we become angry at others and keep that anger seething in our souls, we give control of our emotions to the people we are angry with. We are saying to ourselves, "I will not be happy until this person or these persons change and do right by me." Whenever our happiness depends on someone else besides God, we are in a sad place.

Over two thousand years ago, the philosopher Epictetus said, "Any person capable of angering you becomes your master; he can anger you only when you permit yourself to be disturbed by him."

The key to letting go of anger is learning to forgive. If you have difficulty forgiving, you could read Dick Tibbits's book *Forgive to Live God's Way* or take an anger-management class, and if those do not work, seek professional help.

The Christian perspective says we are all sinners, children of Adam's fallen race, and not one of us is in a position to pass judgment on the other. Were it not for the grace of God, we would be in the same position as the person we are tempted to pass judgment on. If we were born into the same family and grew up under the same circumstances, we probably would be in the same position or worse.

Ultimately it is in accepting God's saving grace and the forgiveness that comes with it that we are restored to him, escape the condemnation from our sin, and become children of God. Receiving his forgiveness is conditioned on our forgiving others as it is stated in Matthew 6, verse 12, "Forgive our sins as we forgive those who sin against us." And in verses 14 and 15 (NIV), it says, "For if you forgive other people when they sin against you, your heavenly Father will also forgive you. But if you do not forgive others their sins, your Father will not forgive your sins."

In opening our hearts to receive God's forgiveness, we open our hearts in forgiveness to others. We are fooling ourselves if we think we can have a saved relationship with God and have an unforgiving spirit (hatred) toward others at the same time. When we allow God to come into our hearts, love comes in with him. As he in love forgives us, we in love forgive others.

Forgiveness does not mean we do not hold people accountable for their deeds; it means we don't carry anger and hatred for them in our hearts. Holding them accountable is at most times the most loving thing we can do for them because we keep them from destroying themselves and others.

For those in government on the opposition side, the natural human leaning is to oppose everything President Trump proposes because of how he and the present Congress disrespected the past president. That would be counterproductive for the country. Ultimately no one wins a war. Some may see themselves as victorious at the end of the conflict, but the casualties and their families pay the price.

All in government are to act in the best interest of the people and to seek to find common ground where possible. The more people taking the high road, the better we will be.

Don't join the haters, for you would become a hater too. We can dislike people's bad ways and still love them and pray for them to become better people. Love always wins in the end.

# THOSE WHO LOVE PRESIDENT TRUMP

The word "love" is used in many ways: there is romantic love, the love of things like food or animals, the love of parents for children, and the love of God. Here the word "love" is being used as a virtue that connotes unselfish loyalty and devotion to the good of another person, such as the love shared between Jonathan and David, which Jonathan acted out in protecting David from his father's (King Saul's) evil desire to kill David by warning him in time so he could escape.

Jonathan helped David escape while knowing that David could one day become king of Israel instead of him. This is the kind of love that makes friendship real and rich with affection but undergirded by respect, concern, and compassion.

If President Trump is to be successful, he needs a lot of prayerful support from loving people. Everyone needs a friend, especially someone in his position with about half the country against him or who at least did not vote for him and some openly hostile toward him. Supportive words and the knowledge that there are people in his corner will provide significant emotional support for him.

To love someone is to be honest with him or her, because trust is the foundation of all good relationships. So it may be necessary at times for friends to disagree with friends or to give them advice they do not want to hear. Because to be a true friend is not to be an ever-ready yes person; you may at times need to be a dissenting voice. Constructive criticism should always be balanced with compliments and encouragement when your friend is heading down the right path.

If the only time you say something to someone it's a negative statement about him or her, that person will automatically dismiss what you have to say, and that approach will definitely jeopardize the relationship.

Here's some advice about giving advice, even to friends: Jesus in the Sermon on the Mount in Matthew 7:1–6 told the people not to judge because as fellow humans we too are imperfect and not in a position to condemn others. As the saying goes, "People in glass houses should not throw stones."

Then he said you should take that huge piece of wood from before your eyes before trying to remove an almost microscopic splinter from your brother's eye.

Our self-protecting mechanisms cause us to quickly reject any negative comments made of us and to view them as attacks on our persons that we need to defend ourselves against. However, for most people criticism is seen as constructive when it comes in the context of a loving relationship, where we feel safe to be vulnerable.

Therefore if we want to provide acceptable constructive criticism and be truly helpful, then we must first cultivate a loving relationship with the person. Otherwise you are viewed as the enemy and rejected as such.

Jesus continued to say you should not give sacred things to dogs or share your jewelry with pigs because they will simply walk over them and come and bite you to pieces. This means there are some people who mean well, and you love them dearly, but they are not in the frame of mind to accept criticism; you are better off leaving them alone because your attempt to help them could result in your own destruction.

There is a difference, though, when you may have to interfere to keep someone from doing bodily harm to himself or herself or to others. In those instances you should be prepared for the repercussions if the person does not take your correction in a good spirit.

It is also a different situation when we are dealing with public figures, as shown in David's experience. The prophet Nathan was sent by God to reprimand him about his act of adultery and murder. I did not get the impression that Nathan and David were bosom buddies, so Nathan used diplomacy and delivered the message in the form of a parable that caused David to condemn himself with his own words.

There are some people who think they love President Trump because they see him as a winner and they cannot stand losers. People who hate losers have problems with self-hate. They see failure or imperfection in themselves and cannot relate to it in a healthy way, so they project it onto others. Haters have great potential for good if they would only learn to love God, themselves, and others.

It is in demanding perfection of others that we most reveal our own imperfections. It is in recognizing our own imperfections that we grasp our common humanity, grow to learn tolerance, and move away from taking the slights of others personally. It is here that we are truly open to be one with God and at peace in our world.

Love is a principle, not only a feeling. Loving someone carries with it a responsibility to help him or her be a better person—not to enable his or her bad ways. Love lifts and empowers both the giver and the receiver to achieve a higher plain of living that brings fulfillment and joy.

# IMPORTANCE OF TRUTH

Philosophers and scientists have differing concepts of what truth is. Those of us who believe in God as the creator have to accept the fact that he who is the originator of all things is the ultimate truth. He has set in place the principles that govern science, the structure of matter, and the results of the interaction of all elements of his creation. This includes what happens in the behavioral realm.

A fundamental truth of God's kingdom is that God is love, and he is calling us into a loving relationship with him. In responding to him, we make choices between love and hate, good and evil, right and wrong, and honesty and dishonesty. Those who identify with God and his rule over his universe embrace with respect the principles he has put in place to govern our interactions.

When a man jumps off a bridge, he meets the truth about gravity, and if he survives the plunge into the water and cannot swim, he faces another truth—that we were not designed to breathe water—and if he is not rescued quickly, that will be the last lesson in truth he will learn in this world.

Similarly, those who break the behavioral laws of God soon find themselves in conflict with the rest of society and sometimes meet a similar fate at the hands of law enforcement and the judicial system. One of God's laws says we should not give false testimony, which means we should speak the truth.

Truthfulness is a fundamental building block for the structure of society. People who are truthful are regarded as honest and trustworthy, essential characteristics for the building of relationships and for positive interactions among people in society.

Why do young people join the armed services? Because they want to be a part of something bigger than themselves, contribute something to nation building, and be prepared for lives of service to their country. What if they find out that at the center of nationhood is a lie, that propounded values are a facade made up simply to impress them, but in reality they are only being used in the grand scheme of some money-loving leaders to grab more for themselves? That love of country, which means love of people, does not really matter because truth, honesty, and integrity don't matter anymore? Relationships don't count, and they will one day become expendable like shell casings on the ground after the battle is over.

Confidence would be lost in our government, and people of integrity wouldn't want to serve our country anymore. Leaders have a great responsibility to act with integrity to give hope and confidence to the future generations of Americans. They do so by being truthful and acting with accountability to the source of all truth—God.

Truthful people have educated consciences because they are honest with themselves about the consequences of their actions, for themselves and others. The opposite is also true—people who are not honest with themselves do not have that inner guiding light that troubles them when they do wrong because their lives are built on self-deception. For such persons, what they feel comfortable with is what they justify as being right.

When politicians make statements that we know are false and we do not seek to hold them accountable but shout with excitement when they spew the lies—whether it is because we belong to the same political party, they hate the same people we hate, or because they support our economic interests—we become enablers of their bad behavior and party to the destruction of society.

Ultimately love wins, and in the end truth will prevail. Unfortunately in the interim there is untold suffering of innocent people at the hands of those who act without consciences educated by the principles of God.

We all love the moment when especially one who is close to us shares his or her true feelings—it creates a moment of authenticity when a person is more real and genuine than ever before. Those treasured moments create stronger relationships and deeper friendships, and they make us feel safe enough to be vulnerable and show our true selves also.

When we are not truthful, we create distrust, which destroys relationships. To restore relationships it takes a lot more time and energy to prove ourselves trustworthy again. Sometimes the falsehood creates such damage that even with great effort some relationships never get back to where they were before.

When people working together are not truthful to each other, it creates an environment of disunity since truthfulness is a prerequisite for trust. There is no unity where there is no trust. Where there is no trust, it's every man for himself. People spend too much time covering their backs because they cannot trust coworkers and fear they may get blamed for things they did not do or that someone else may take the credit for their good work.

The best leaders know how to build a good team because good teamwork multiplies effectiveness exponentially.

When workers realize that the organization they are working for is built on lies, such as false advertising, unsubstantiated claims, defective products, or erroneous projections, they become concerned about the stability of the organization and their future employment status.

It is difficult to give your best or to live with a clear conscience knowing that the organization you are working for is not genuine but deceiving the public with nonfunctional or substandard products or services.

When an organization has leaders who are truthful, honest, and upright, its employees feel safe and can give their best, knowing that promises will be kept and that they will receive credit and appreciation for what they do. In that kind of environment, people usually find such fulfillment that they are willing to go above and beyond what is required to ensure success.

People who deal with issues they are afraid to face by lying usually find themselves lying to cover other lies, creating a downward spiral for the soul. Lying and living a lie create a life of fear, fear of discovery when the truth is revealed and the fantasy image we have created of ourselves crumbles, fear that we will be exposed, naked before the world in unbearable shame.

Those who are constantly untruthful after some time cannot distinguish between what is factual and what is not. Things get muddled in their minds to the point where they begin to believe the lies they themselves have told. That departure from reality heads down the road toward insanity.

The path of truth is a much better way. Accept the reality that God has set things to work in the world according to his character. To accept him and his principles in our lives brings the light of his presence, which dispels the darkness of our souls.

The life of truth is a life of faith, that inner confidence that says, "God loves us and he has our backs, so when we speak the truth, we are doing what he wants, and he will protect us against the consequences we fear." Those who genuinely love us will appreciate our honesty and not turn their backs on us in our vulnerable moments.

# LESSONS FROM RULERS PAST

George Santayana, twentieth-century philosopher, essayist, poet, and novelist, shared the thought that when we forget the past, we will repeat in our lives its missteps all over again. Not that history is by any means a perfect predictor of the future. If that were the case, how could we account for the advances we have made over the years?

Looking at the past allows us to gain wisdom without the pain of going through undesirable experiences ourselves. Benjamin Franklin puts it this way: "Experience keeps a dear school, but fools will learn in no other."

History does give us a base for creating understanding of our world, ourselves, and the interactions between God and man in the past, and all of this has implications for the future. There are certainly things that have happened in the past that we would not want to see happen again, and there are some good things that we would want to see over and over again.

The path of progress centers on preserving and building on what is good and functional and changing that which does not serve our best interests. Neither perpetual sameness nor constant change is our reality. History helps us take a good look at the similarities of our human tendencies to those of our predecessors and inspires us to make better choices going forward.

Here are some of the great and not so great rulers and leaders of the past. Let's see what lessons we can learn from them.

# MOSES

Moses was born to a Hebrew (Israelite) family in Egypt at a time when his people were slaves to the Egyptians. Even under the oppression of slavery, their number kept increasing, which made Pharaoh, ruler of Egypt, fearful that they would become so numerous that they would be a threat to his kingdom. He ordered that all male children born to Hebrew women should be thrown into the Nile River.

Moses's parents hid him at home as long as they could, and when they could keep him there no longer, they made a waterproof basket, put him in it, and in the day hid him among the reeds on the Nile with his older sister watching him. He was found by Pharaoh's daughter, who decided to adopt him. Moses's sister, who saw Pharaoh's daughter discover the baby, volunteered to find a nanny for the baby. The princess agreed, and Moses was taken home, where he was cared for until he was older.

He grew up in the lap of privilege with the education and exposure that it affords, but he never forgot who his people were. One day he saw an Egyptian beating a Hebrew, went to his rescue, killed the Egyptian, and hid his body in the sand. The next day he tried to settle a quarrel between two Hebrews, and the aggressor asked him if he was going to kill him like he killed the Egyptian.

Moses, realizing that his deed was known, fled for his life to Midian. There he joined the family of Jethro, the priest of Midian, married one of his daughters, and spent years herding sheep. It took seeming failure and herding sheep to teach Moses humility and patience, character traits necessary for good leadership.

Now he was ready to lead God's people God's way. God called to him at the experience of the burning bush in the wilderness and sent him to confront the new pharaoh with God's request to let his people go. With the moving of the mighty hand of God, he led the children of Israel out of Egypt into the wilderness on the way to the Promised Land.

In the wilderness the Israelites tested Moses's patience over and over because they were an ungrateful, rebellious, and complaining lot. The love Moses had for them kept him pleading with God not to destroy them but to give them another chance.

Another outstanding quality that Moses had was his willingness to take advice. A prime example was the occasion when his father-in-law, Jethro, visited with him in the wilderness. Jethro observed that Moses spent most of his time as a judge settling disputes for the people, working at it from morning till night. Jethro advised him to choose honest men and teach them the laws and principles of God and then set up a multitier judicial system, allowing only the most difficult cases to come to him. Moses took Jethro's advice, thereby learning to delegate, and saved himself for more important work.

If you think helping people improve their lots in life will always result in expression of appreciation and gratitude, remember Moses and the children of Israel. He was successful because he had a clear vision of where God wanted him to lead his people and the principles God wanted him to use in getting them there. Moses put God first in his life and was a true servant leader and is revered as one of the greatest leaders ever.

# SAUL AND DAVID

After Israel settled in Palestine under the leadership of Joshua, there was no central government. Tribal leaders and elders provided leadership for the people. Whenever there was a national threat, God would raise up a judge who would lead the nation to deal with whatever external or internal challenge they were facing. By the time of Samuel, who was judge, priest, and prophet, the people of Israel wanted a king like the nations around them. Samuel warned them that a king would make servants out of them and exact taxes, but they would not listen. So God instructed Samuel to give them a king.

He anointed Saul, a tall and handsome man, as king. Saul was the kind of person who fit the profile the Israelites were looking for and did well for a while, until his character flaws and mental illness began to show.

Samuel, instructed by God, anointed David secretly to be Saul's successor. Saul, unaware of this, engaged the services of David as musician to play the lyre for him as a means of soothing his spirit. He also appointed David to be one of his armor bearers. In this move God orchestrated for David to be at court and learn by observation the systems of governance for the kingdom.

In time David becomes active in Saul's army and becomes a very successful military figure in the nation. Saul becomes jealous of David and fears David's popularity with the people will lead to David's ascendancy to the throne instead of his son Jonathan.

In his determination not to let this happen, Saul tries to kill David. After several attempts on his life, David escapes and goes into hiding to save his own life. Saul was bent on committing murder because what he wanted was more important to him than what God wanted.

On one occasion of Saul's pursuit of David, David hid in a cave. Saul chose the same cave to take a rest. While he was resting, David went near him unnoticed and cut off a piece of his robe. After Saul left the cave, David came out and called to him, showing him the piece of robe and letting him know that he could have killed him but spared his life because he would not harm the Lord's anointed.

David knew that God had appointed Saul as king, and it was not for him, David, to undo that decision. There are some things that are to be left for God to take care of, in his way and in his time. David must have also been conscious that he too was anointed to be king of Israel, and the way he treated the reigning king would set the precedent as to how he should be treated when he took on the role of king.

As Saul got older, he drifted further and further from God, choosing to do things as he pleased rather than as God instructed. On one occasion he was preparing for battle, and as customary, Saul and the soldiers waited for the priest to offer a sacrifice to seek God's favor before going into battle. Samuel was late in coming; Saul got impatient and offered the sacrifice himself. This was unacceptable to God because Saul was not a priest. God rejected Saul because he would not walk in God's way.

Many of Saul's actions were driven by his fear, not his faith. He drifted so far from God that nearing the end of his reign, he resorted to consulting the Witch of Endor. Saul died shortly after in battle with the Philistines.

David's reign was better than Saul's but not perfect. He succumbed to his human weakness and committed adultery and then murder in an attempt to cover it up, but when confronted by the prophet Nathan, he humbled himself before God, repented of his sin, and asked God for forgiveness and a transformed heart. He was blessed with a restored relationship with God and in the end was referred to as a man after God's own heart.

Some may wonder how a man as violent as David could be referred to as being so close to God. Looking at that entire period, almost everywhere you looked, there was violence—oppressive violent slavery in Egypt, skirmishes along the way as they traveled through the wilderness, and the violence they created as they dislodged the occupants of Palestine.

After they settled in the Promised Land, there were raiding parties from surrounding nations taking crops at harvest time and men, women, and children as slaves. There was also outright invasion and the attempt to subjugate the whole nation. It was a time to kill or be killed; if they could not fight, they could not survive.

While God hates violence and human suffering, he does not suddenly, radically change the norms of society. He allows us to learn and grow from our successes and failures. He works with us to build and develop our characters and systems over time. Remember he made time and is not limited by it. His plan has no haste or delay.

# SOLOMON AND REHOBOAM—A KINGDOM DIVIDED

By the end of David's reign, most of Israel's nearby enemies were either engulfed into the Davidic kingdom or subdued. Before his death he appointed his son Solomon as his successor. When Solomon became king, God told him to make a request of him. Solomon asked God for wisdom. God granted his request and promised him prosperity and wealth with it.

Solomon fulfilled his father's request and his divine responsibility by building a temple in Jerusalem to the glory of God and the pride of the nation. Solomon became an icon in his country, renowned at home and abroad for his great wisdom.

Like his father, he too had expansionist ambitions. However, he was not a man of the sword but a man of diplomacy. He cut a number of deals with the surrounding nations that brought him great wealth and power. Unfortunately he used a method common in the culture at the time of taking one of the other rulers' daughters as one of his wives to seal the deal.

His close affiliation with and affection for idolatrous women led him to lose sight of the close relationship he should have maintained with God. He turned from the principle of God and failed to respect and care for the nation entrusted to him. In his quest to expand his wealth and power, he became very oppressive to his people.

Solomon had a golden opportunity to build on the progress his father had made in exalting the worship of God and making it dominant in the nation. Israel was attracted to the idol-worshiping practices of its neighbors, but under David these practices were not allowed to rise to dominance. As Solomon sank into idolatry, so did the nation.

Solomon appointed his son Rehoboam to succeed him after his death. When Rehoboam was about to ascend to the throne, the people met at Shechem to confirm him in the position. There, before his inauguration, the tribal elders asked him if he would lessen the yoke of oppression his father, Solomon, had placed on them.

The relationship between the tribe of Judea and the ten tribes to the north was tenuous at best, and they were not happy that David, a Judean, replaced Saul as king. David had skillfully avoided conflict with his brother to the north, but Solomon's oppression had strained the relationship, and they were near their breaking point.

Rehoboam asked for three days to consider the matter and bring them an answer. They agreed and dispersed to their homes. Rehoboam sought advice, first from the senior men who were advisers to his father. They told him to give them a favorable answer, so they would remain loyal to him. Next he asked his contemporaries, his friends whom he grew up with, and they gave him the opposite advice.

When the three days passed and the people assembled again, Rehoboam told them that their burdens would be heavier and not lighter as they requested. At that response the ten northern tribes rejected Rehoboam, and he was made king over only the tribes of Judea and Benjamin.

Rehoboam grew up in the lap of luxury, disconnected from the day-to-day suffering of the common people, and surrounded himself with people of similar social standing. He did not have the emotional intelligence to recognize the best course of action for his own good and the good of the nation. He took the people for granted, and they rejected him.

The ten northern tribes chose Jeroboam to be their king; the kingdom was divided because Rehoboam placed self-interest above the interest of the people. He did not learn that leaders are servants of the people. They put up kings and take them down.

The history related to the ten northern tribes, referred to as Israel, from here on took a downward turn as they became steeped in idolatry and drifted further and further from God. God withdrew his protection from them, and they were taken into captivity, never to be reconstituted as a nation again.

# AHAZ AND ISAIAH—FAITH IN MAN OR GOD

Almost two hundred years after Rehoboam, King Ahaz reigned as king of Judea. Jerusalem was under attack from the king of Aram (Syria), supported by the king of Israel. God sent the prophet Isaiah to tell King Ahaz that they would not succeed, and as an assurance of that, Ahaz should ask God for a sign.

Ahaz refused to ask God for a sign because his faith was not in God but in an alliance he had formed with Assyria. The prophet told him that if he did not stand firm in faith, he would not stand at all. When rulers do not want to listen to God, they do so at their own peril. As promised, God did deliver Jerusalem from the attack, and Assyria later became a thorn in Judea's side.

In contrast, Hezekiah, the grandson of Ahaz, turned to God in prayer when he had a similar problem. Sennacherib, king of Assyria, threatened to attack Jerusalem. After Hezekiah prayed asking for deliverance, God sent the prophet Isaiah to tell him that he would receive what he asked for and the Assyrians would not shoot an arrow against Jerusalem.

Before the Assyrians could attack, 185,000 of his men died in one night. Sennacherib returned to Nineveh and never returned to Palestine. Sometime after, he was killed by two of his sons while he was worshiping in the temple of his god Nisroch.

It is interesting that Hezekiah went to the temple of his God, prayed for deliverance, and received it. Sennacherib went to the temple of his god and was killed by his own sons.

# NEBUCHADNEZZAR AND CYRUS

After Hezekiah, his son Manasseh reigned. He was an evil king, desecrating the temple and leading Judea deep into idolatry to the extent of offering human sacrifices. After a brief reform by King Josiah, Judea plunged back into its evil, idolatrous ways.

God had promised through the prophets that if they did not change their ways, he would use Nebuchadnezzar, King of Babylon, to punish them, and so he did. After several invasions the Babylonians killed or carried off as captives most of the Judean population, leaving behind a few poor people.

In Babylon God tried to use some of the faithful of Judea to share knowledge of him with Nebuchadnezzar, but he was a slow learner. First he had a dream that troubled him, but he could not remember the dream, so he called for the magicians and wise men to tell him his dream and its interpretation. Of course they could have conjured up an interpretation, but to tell him a dream he had and could not remember was beyond them.

He threatened to kill them all, but before the execution date, Daniel came to the rescue. Daniel was a Judean exile in the king's service who was considered a wise man. God told Daniel the dream and the interpretation. He shared the information with Nebuchadnezzar, who verified that that was the exact dream he'd had.

In the dream he saw an image of a man made up of multiple metals, and the interpretation stated that Babylon was represented by the head of gold, and that other nations, represented by the other metals, would rule after Babylon was moved off the scene. He was impressed with Daniel's god, thanked Daniel, and rewarded him with a promotion.

As time passed and he mulled over the interpretation of the dream, it did not sit well with him. He wanted his dynasty to last forever, so he came up with a plan to change the future from how God told him it was going to go.

He constructed an image of gold from head to foot, in contrast to the one he had seen in the dream, which was of different kinds of metal. He was sending Daniel's god a message that the future would not be as he'd predicted in the dream, but Babylon was going to rule forever. The image of Nebuchadnezzar's creation did not just have a head of gold; instead, the entire image was of gold.

He had the massive structure, ninety feet high and nine feet wide, installed on the plain of Dura and ordered that on the date and at the time appointed, all officials of his kingdom were to attend the dedication of the image. He further ordered that when the sound of music was heard playing, everyone was to bow down and worship the image.

There were three faithful worshipers of God present, who were working by God's plan for their future, not Nebuchadnezzar's, and they would not bow down. The penalty for not bowing down was to be thrown into a furnace prepared for the purpose. The three Hebrew men were Judean exiles also, and they were determined to be faithful to their God.

Nebuchadnezzar decided to give them a second chance to bow down to his image, but they made it clear to him that they would never bow down to any of his gods. They informed him that they believed that their God would deliver them, but if he chose not to, they still would not bow down.

The king became even more furious and ordered the furnace heated seven times hotter. Some of the king's strongest soldiers threw the three faithful into the furnace. The furnace was so hot that it killed the soldiers who threw the men in, but nothing happened to the three Hebrew men.

Nebuchadnezzar noticed that there were four men alive and well in the furnace, and the fourth looked like a son of the gods. It most likely was an angel sent by God to protect his children. The king called them out and acknowledged that their god was great and ordered that everybody in his kingdom worship the god of the Hebrews.

Despite all the evidence before him, Nebuchadnezzar continued on his path of arrogance and self-centeredness. It was common among the rulers of his day to think of themselves as being endowed with divine attributes. If he thought of himself as a god, it would be difficult for him to come to the place where he humbled himself before God.

His third opportunity came when he had another dream that troubled him. This time he remembered the dream but could not find among his magicians anyone to give him the interpretation, until Daniel, the chief of the wise men, came and was able to give him the interpretation.

In his dream the king saw a huge tree, reaching to the sky, full of beautiful leaves and fruits that supplied food for all. It was a shelter to animals, and birds made their nests in its branches. Then he saw a heavenly messenger instructing that the tree should be cut down, but the stump should be preserved with an iron and bronze band around it for seven years.

In interpreting the dream, Daniel told the king that the tree represented him, that God had issued a decree against him. He would take himself away from people and live like a wild animal, becoming wet with the dew and eating grass like a cow. The stump remaining meant that his life would be preserved until he acknowledged that God rules.

Daniel advised Nebuchadnezzar to turn from his sins and wickedness, do what was right, and show kindness to the oppressed. God would see it and possibly allow his prosperity to continue. He did not heed the warning, and a year later, while he was admiring the beautiful city he had built, in his haughtiness he proclaimed, "Is not this the great Babylon I have built as the royal residence, by my mighty power and for the glory of my majesty?" (Daniel 4:30 NIV.)

As he uttered those words, the prophecy was fulfilled in him—he left the palace, went into the field, and ate grass like a cow for seven years. At the end of the seven years, his sanity returned, and he gave praise to God.

This is a well-documented case of a monarch suffering from a severe mental illness. The condition still exists today. It is called Boanthropy, a real mental disorder that causes the victims to take on the appearance, habits, and posture of cattle.

Nebuchadnezzar's experience shows that God will use the action of one ruler or nation to punish or bring to justice another who has gone too far in wickedness, but that does not mean he will not hold accountable the ones he uses.

The turning of the tide for the Babylonian empire came one night during the reign of Nebuchadnezzar's grandson Belshazzar. He was having a party with a thousand of his nobles and ordered that the vessels that were taken from the temple in Jerusalem be brought in. He and his guests drank wine from the vessels in disrespect of the god of the Jewish people.

In the midst of their revelry, there appeared a hand writing in the plaster on the palace wall. Belshazzar became frightened, and his knees began to shake. When he got the interpretation of what was written, it said, "You are weighed in the balance and found wanting."

That night the combined forces of the Medes and Persians breached Babylon's defenses, captured the city, and executed Belshazzar. Cyrus, the conquering monarch, gave the Jewish people permission to return to Jerusalem and rebuild the city walls and temple. This had been prophesied by Isaiah over 150 years before.

In Isaiah's prophecy (Isaiah chapter 44), God calls Cyrus "his shepherd," and in Jeremiah's prophecy, he calls Nebuchadnezzar "his servant." These were two pagan kings, one used by God to punish the Jewish people and the other to restore them. They were not kings like David, who was after God's own heart.

They were used, much as you use a tool for a purpose until you are done with it, and not endorsed, as someone you take into your family. Leaders who wish to be endorsed by God and blessed to produce the greatest good possible in their tenure must be humbly surrendered to God and reflect his principles in their lives.

God will use anyone in a position of leadership for the greater good of humanity, as far as he or she allows him to. For example, an unconverted preacher can preach a good sermon because God sees the congregation needs it. They leave church full, and he stays empty.

# MAHATMA GANDHI (1869–1948)

Gandhi emerged as a force to be reckoned with in India's struggle for independence from British colonial rule. His work in the movement against oppression started when he helped with the struggle of Indians to gain equality in South Africa while working there as an attorney at law.

While in South Africa, he developed the approach of using nonviolence and passive resistance as a means of stimulating change. Learning from the successes achieved there, he utilized the same methodologies in India.

At first it was organizing peasant farmers against the oppressive policy of British landlords who compelled the peasants to grow indigo, which was declining in price, and at the same time forcing them to sell the crops at a price the landlords fixed. Gandhi organized the farmers, who in block refused to work under those conditions. The landlords relented, and the people won.

Gandhi's successful intervention caused his methods to gain the respect of the Indian people, from whom he gained great support for the salt march to protest the British tax on salt (reminiscent of the Boston Tea Party).

His success was in part due to his openness to all people, including women. His inclusiveness enabled him to unite opposing religious factions (Muslims and Hindus) in the nonviolent effort for independence.

He concluded that the British were holding India in its grasp because Indians were helping them. He encouraged his fellow countrymen to practice civil disobedience by not cooperating with the British colonial infrastructure or working for them. He encouraged the boycott of British goods and institutions, including schools.

The movement he created brought the British Empire to its knees, and India gained its independence in 1947, without his instructing his followers to fire a single bullet. His approach to life was more Christlike than that of many professed Christians in his country at that time.

The British, in the era of Britain's colonial rule, took their churches with them but for the most part not the Christ of the church. That era did immeasurable damage to the Christian faith because although they carried with them the name Christian, their governing practices were rapacious, racist, segregationist, oppressive, and unjust.

They had such powerful influence around the world; there was a time when this song was sung:

> When Britain first, at Heaven's command
> Arose from out the azure main;
> This was the charter of the land,

> And guardian angels sang this strain:
> Rule, Britannia! Rule the waves:
> Britons never will be slaves.

While they abhorred slavery for themselves, they had no problem inflicting it on other people, until those of conscience in their midst rose up against it and fought for and won the abolition of slavery.

A nation that was among the first to see the translations of the Bible into its native language and sent missionaries like Livingston around the world failed in its stewardship to God and is now reduced to a nation struggling with nationalism, cutting itself off from the rest of Europe.

A nation that opens itself to the rest of the world is open for the blessings of God. A closed hand cannot receive anything. Greed and selfishness are the downfall of any people. Self-sacrificing love is the path to a great future.

The United States must be careful in pursuing a policy of nationalism lest it become so insular that it loses its influence for good in the world. The United States has become great because so many talented people have come to it from all over the world bringing the skills and the drive to create better lives for themselves and their children.

It is interesting that a country of descendants of immigrants has become a country that is anti-immigration. There is nothing wrong with a country protecting its borders and controlling the rate of influx of immigrants, but to have a politically generated anti-immigrant fervor is counterproductive to the nation's spiritual well-being and its future prosperity.

When we forget where we are coming from, we forget the God who brought us this far, and we seek to go forward in our own strength and wisdom. That is a prescription for failure. This is a land to which some came to exercise their religious freedom, and others came for a second chance for a better economic future. Have we become so selfish that we want to deny others those same opportunities?

# ADOLF HITLER (1889–1945)

After dropping out of high school in 1905, Hitler lived in Vienna, at the time a place of increasing religious prejudice and racism. While there, he saw Mayor Karl Lueger use anti-Semitic rhetoric for political gain. He was also influenced there by Georg Ritter von Schönerer, an advocate of German nationalism who was against Jews, Slavs, and Catholics.

Hitler enlisted and fought in the German Army during the First World War and loved it. He was very disappointed when Germany lost the war, and he, along with others, blamed the defeat on Marxists and civilian leaders who they felt had stabbed the army in the back.

After the war he got involved in politics and rose to the head of the National Socialist German Workers' Party. He developed as a skillful orator and was comfortable speaking before large audiences.

He showed his great love of power when he attempted a coup in Bavaria. After his arrest he was tried and sentenced to prison. While in prison he wrote a book in which he outlined his ideology and his plans to transform Germany into a race-based society.

When Hitler was released from prison in 1924, the German economy had rebounded, and there was not much room for agitated politics. He became involved in politics again and became very active after the collapse of the US stock market in November 24, 1929, ushering in the Great Depression. The Germany economy was hit hard, millions lost their jobs, and several banks failed.

Hitler and his party capitalized on the downturn in the economy, promising to strengthen the country's crumbling financial state, turn things around, and create jobs. They also promised to renounce the Versailles Treaty, which required Germany to pay for war damages from the First World War.

His campaign also carried strong nationalistic tones that pitted the German people against Jews and others he could blame for the troubles of the country, with cunning lies to create fear and anger in the minds of the people already perturbed about their economic plight.

Through a series of moves, he exploited and manipulated the volatile and chaotic situation until he was appointed chancellor. Surrounding himself with people of like minds, he intensified his power base. Along the way he was systematically eliminating the opposition parties.

When he had built a strong enough power base, he had legislation passed that made him dictator of the country, promising beforehand that President Paul von Hindenburg would retain veto powers—a promise he did not keep. From there he moved to get rid of the rest of his political opponents. He fulfilled his dream of becoming a fascist dictator like Mussolini in Italy.

He and his Nazi Party systematically dismantled the free press, only allowing those who were a part of his propaganda machinery to remain open. This was effective in keeping the public from knowing the true direction he was taking the country and leaving no one to keep him accountable.

His rise to power plunged the world into the darkness of World War II, an era of genocide for Jews and other ethnic minorities, the loss of millions of lives, and untold suffering around the world. For him it ended in suicide.

The grabbing after power for the sake of feeling powerful usually comes from an effort to compensate for intense feelings of inferiority. In that kind of mind, there is little or no room for empathy and compassion, which are needed to care for and service the needs of others. The good they do is all in an effort to feed their egos and make them look good to the public.

During the Second World War, a study was done of Hitler by psychologist Henry A. Murray. He concluded that Hitler suffered from pathological narcissism. The closest modern equivalent to pathological narcissism we have is narcissistic personality disorder.

People with narcissistic personality disorder are overly important to themselves, making them conceited, arrogant, and boastful; they become upset when they do not get the admiration and attention they think they deserve. While they lack empathy for others, belittling those they perceive as inferior to them, they have self-esteem problems that make them vulnerable to the slightest criticism.

Unfortunately people with this kind of disorder do not easily accept that anything can be wrong with them. Usually the opportunity to get them to seek help comes when the condition progresses to depression resulting from their perceived rejection or criticism they cannot handle.

Hitler was the master of manipulating chaotic situations. In the midst of chaos, fear is heightened, and people in fear lose reasoning and make irrational decisions. Watch out for those who seek to create chaos or who thrive in a chaotic environment—they are the masters of devious manipulations and the destroyers of civil society.

People make up the nation, so to participate in nation building, we must be involved in building people. When a leader puts down one set of his people and overemphasizes another set, he creates people with inferiority and superiority complexes, which is divisive and unhealthy for nation building.

Playing the race or religion card was not something to be taken lightly. It seemed that many people innocently looked the other way because of anti-immigrant statements he made. But Hitler's ideas along these lines were tolerated far too long by well-meaning Germans, and when they realized that they had a monster on their hands, it was too late to turn the movement back. It took a world war in which millions of lives were lost to stop it.

While in the progressive business world we talk of servant leadership, emotional intelligence, human capital, and the speed of trust, our recent politics is reminiscent of the old world of manipulation, authoritarianism, and rulership that is Machiavellian at times.

The system of government in the United States today does not allow for easy transition to dictatorship, but the energy spent trying to control someone who wants to move in that direction is counterproductive to nation building.

Hitler was not born a monster. He developed in reaction to the abusive relationship he had with his father. His self-protecting mechanisms chipped in, giving him this overwhelming desire to control his world to keep pain from coming to him again. Those who are abusing their children could be creating monsters for themselves and the rest of the world. It is so much better to love our children and through them give a gift of goodness to the world.

The countries that fought the tyranny of Hitler for the most part did not fully learn the lesson of the horrors of tyranny. After World War II, France and Britain retained control of colonies at times by extremely violent, repressive means, costing thousands of lives. The United States maintained Jim Crow laws in the South that were oppressive to African Americans there.

The long, hard struggle for freedom from oppression continued around the world, and free people of conscience of all races moved by the Spirit of God struggled to create in our world a more just society.

One of the moves anti-Semites of Hitler's day used in their attempt to turn Christians against Jews was to blame Jews for crucifying Christ. If they knew the mission and purpose of Christ, they would realize that he allowed himself to be crucified to pay the penalty for our sins so that we could come to know the love of God and be empowered to love all humans—including those who crucified him.

While dying on the cross, Christ asked God, the Father, to forgive those who put him there because he knew they were acting out of their envy and desire to preserve their status in society. Their fear and hate created a blindness of their souls that kept them from seeing the beauty of innocence, and they could not recognize the depths of what they were doing.

Ultimately love will win over selfishness and hate because God is too awesome and powerful to be a loser. We see in his love the greatness of his kingdom, and in the hate of mortals, the weakness of their souls.

# NELSON MANDELA (1918–2013)

Mandela was an attorney in Johannesburg who joined the African National Congress (ANC), a political party that fought for the rights of black South Africans. He was involved in the organizing and operations of the youth arm of the ANC and was a key figure in the fight against apartheid.

Throughout the years of both Dutch and British rule of South Africa, the country always practiced segregation by ethnicity. During the Second World War, the shortage of white workers created the opportunity for many black workers to move into urban areas. After the war the government faced the challenge of having a much larger population in its urban center without the appropriate infrastructure to facilitate it.

With the war over, the white working class began to complain about the shortage of employment opportunities, blaming blacks for taking the jobs at lower pay. They also felt threatened by the agitation of blacks for participation in the political process.

As the country approached general elections in 1948, the National Party convinced the predominantly white electorate that the ruling United Party was too liberal to deal with the issues at hand and that they would protect their interest with a system of apartheid.

Notice that when economic difficulties arise, those who are self-centered look first to disenfranchise others so that they may retain their privileged position and continue to benefit irrespective of what happens to the rest of the population. Again the forces of darkness exploit crises.

After the United Party won the election, they went full force into the implementation of their apartheid policy, and by 1950 had laws enforcing the total separation of the population by race. These laws made interracial marriages illegal, protected certain jobs for whites only, classified the population by ethnicity, designated homelands for each ethnic group, and forcibly relocated over 3.5 million non-white South Africans from their homes into segregated neighborhoods.

The government empowered its army and police to enforce the new laws and suppressed opposition with rigor, which created misery, mayhem, and death for many black South Africans. It was a reign of terror.

The changes cut across all aspects of societal life from separate schools and universities down to which bench you could sit on in the park. The facilities for blacks were always inferior to those for whites.

This is the South Africa that Nelson Mandela and many others devoted their lives to change. He became a well-known activist and organizer against apartheid and was arrested several times and charged with sedition without being convicted until 1962.

The ANC pursued a nonviolent approach, at first using marches and strikes as protests. The police became increasingly violent toward protesters. In 1960 at a protest against pass laws (blacks were required to have passes to move about), police killed sixty-nine people and injured many others.

The brutality stimulated many other protests around the country, and the government responded by banning the opposition organizations, including the ANC and the Pan Africanist Congress. Both organizations went underground and created organizations that would respond with violence.

Mandela was arrested in 1962 for inciting workers' strikes and leaving the country without permission. He was convicted and sentenced to five years in prison. While serving that sentence, he was charged with conspiring to overthrow the state.

He used his trial as a platform for arguing his case against apartheid. He was eventually convicted and sentenced to life imprisonment along with other leaders opposed to apartheid.

Life in prison was rough for Mandela, but he survived it for twenty-seven years, until he was released in 1990. He remained faithful to his commitment to do all he could to free his people from the oppression of apartheid. He was a moderate politician, skillful negotiator, and a beacon of hope for many.

The South African government came under immense pressure from the international community to end apartheid, There were sanctions by other countries that affected South Africa's economy. The United Nations tried from the early 1960s to create pressure on South Africa but did not receive support from Western block nations, who feared that Mandela's alleged ties to South Africa's Communist Party would turn the tide there toward communism in the height of the Cold War.

There were also economic interests: many corporations, institutions, and individuals from the United Kingdom, France, and the United States had investments in South Africa or in companies that did business there. We see this repeated in history where economic interests take precedence over human rights.

As the atrocities of the South African police against protesters received publicity in the United States, they kindled a grassroots opposition that found expression among faith-based organizations and especially on university campuses by students and teachers. They joined in the effort to get universities and other entities to divest their investments in South Africa.

Their efforts were met with success, with the biggest hit coming from the University of California, which pulled $3 billion. The US government followed after, with Congress passing the Comprehensive Anti-Apartheid Act in 1986.

With pressure building internally and externally, by 1990 the South African government was now ready to make changes. The path forward was not clear, nor would it be an easy walk. There were many challenging issues to deal with, including what would become of the minority white population should the majority black citizens take control of government.

Mandela did not come out of prison bitter and angry but with a heart of forgiveness. He was conscious of what he was up against and the damage that had been done but was visionary enough to see beyond that, what a healed South Africa would be like.

He was also keenly aware of the damage he would do to himself if he kept bitterness in his heart—he saw it as poison and a hindrance to what he needed to accomplish for his country. He did not want to be kept in the mental prison of hate.

Mandela played a pivotal role in the negotiations that led to the creation of an interim constitution, which included provision for a government of national unity coming out of the first general election for the country that included all its people. Mandela's party, the ANC, won, and he became the next president of South Africa. He kept his promise to create an integrated government.

His administration worked for reconciliation between racial groups in the country and the creation of the Truth and Reconciliation Commission for the investigation of past human-rights abuses and the granting of amnesty for some offenders.

There were many who wanted Mandela killed before and while he was in prison, but God preserved his life for the great work he had planned for him. Post-Mandela South Africa is not perfect, but there is hope, and that hope will shine brighter if its leaders and people adopt the principles of the kingdom of God and move away from violence and corruption.

After centuries of oppression, it will take some time, forgiveness, and character growth to forge a greater nation. Thank God they are now free to do that.

There is something that President Mandela could not have done and President Trump cannot do, and that is to give character to the people. A leader can be inspirational and point people in the right direction, but each person decides how he or she will relate to the world.

Mandela, like many other great leaders, by the grace of God, has done his part for his country and the world. What future will we leave for our children?

# THE CHALLENGE FOR CHRISTIAN LEADERSHIP IN TODAY'S WORLD

Spiritual leaders have always played a critical role in guiding nations to choose ethical values and in leading young and old alike in the principles of the kingdom of God. Whenever they fail at this task, we see societies plunge into decadence and moral decline.

Whenever the prophets of old failed to warn the people about injustice and the need to care for the vulnerable of society and instead whitewashed the deeds of their wicked friends for personal gain, then they and their friends usually perished together.

There has been a lot of effort by some religious leaders to push for the election of individuals who reflect their views on specific issues without recognizing that when they associate with politicians too closely, they are at risk of bringing dishonor to the name of God.

It is not enough to support persons for elected office because they are for or against particular views on governance. There are some other critical questions to ask, such as whether they are truthful, have a history of treating people with respect, can be reasoned with, and have integrity.

The country will not become moral because we have legislators who pass laws that we favor. Morality cannot be legislated. The country will increase in morality as its citizens come to know and respect the source of moral power, God, and are transformed by him.

Involvement in the legislative process can be very important in pursuing the principles of the kingdom of God and the common good of all. We should spend more time, effort, and money modeling and teaching the principles of the kingdom of God and less on politicians. Most of them have developed the skill of saying what they know we want to hear from them so they can get our support and who in the end do not model in their lives respect, decency, and morality before the nation.

When we support candidates for elected office, we should not be so tied to them that we cannot hold them accountable and call them out when they are taking the wrong course for the greater good of the nation.

Too often we shout "hurrah" when politicians share our pet peeves and keep silent when they are rude and disrespectful to others or show disregard for the poor, vulnerable, and disenfranchised of society. We do not solve problems by destroying people—that's the mentality that put Christ on the cross.

When we knowingly support corrupt candidates for office simply because they share our views on one issue and do not care about the havoc they will create, we forget that the end does not justify the means. God is in charge of the world, and we do not have to resort to underhanded means to further his kingdom. Let us use his methods, and let him take care of the end results. He is quietly capable.

If as a Christian leader, you do not have love for all people, bowels of compassion, and empathy for the vulnerable and suffering souls in our society, you are in the wrong place. Ask God for a change of heart that you may become like Jesus or find another place to work.

The stability and progress of the United States are significant for the growth of the Christian church. The United States has been the modern cradle of the Christian faith. From these shores, missionaries have gone around the world to improve literacy, health care, and access to food and clean water—and with those, they bring knowledge of a loving and caring God.

In times of natural disasters or other events that create humanitarian crises, faith-based organizations in this country have played a significant role along with our government in relief efforts. We do not want to get to the place where the inner workings of our government become so distasteful to the rest of the world that they hinder our ability to do such great work.

Time and time again, our loving God has placed in the hearts of those with means the willingness to use their resources to help those in need around the world. While we should not fail to care for the needy in our own country, our hearts must still burn with compassion for the difficulties others face around the world.

# JESUS CHRIST AS A LEADER

There are people who have provided great leadership in this world without an official national or ecclesiastical title for the major part of their work on earth. The greatest of these is Jesus Christ. This divine-incarnate man grew up in humble surroundings away from the pomp and circumstance of life among the aristocracy.

By the time he was an adult, his mother, fraught with the consciousness of his divine origin and the evidence she had seen in his growing-up years, challenged him to perform his first public miracle at a wedding feast at Cana in Galilee. While they were at the wedding feast, all the wine was consumed before the feast was over, a rather embarrassing situation for the couple and their family.

Jesus's mother told him the wine was gone and asked him to do something about it. He instructed the servants to fill six thirty-gallon water jars with water and serve it to the guests. When the master of the banquet tasted the water, it turned to wine, and he complimented it as the best and asked why they saved it till last.

His first miracle was not to create a mountain of gold, a private stash from which to fund the building of an earthly kingdom; it was a kind act to add to the joy of a festive occasion and to make the newlyweds and their family happy.

This first miracle set the tone of his life's ministry. It identified the nature of his mission. The mission of a person or organization encapsulates the character of his or her cause, the purpose for which he or she exists, and the guiding light that will carry him or her forward.

As a leader, his life had the following key characteristics:

1. Humility

He was not engaged in unnecessary self-promotion and did not put others down for the purpose of exalting himself but instead showed equal respect for people of all walks of life and was free of arrogance and the self-important trappings that usually accompany people of status and accomplishment in this world.

Humility is a strength, not a weakness; it frees the soul to move away from its crippling self-centeredness, giving it freedom to see the world's reality with clarity.

2. Kindness

He did not look down on those who were ignorant but lifted them by teaching them a better way of living. His teaching was not just lecture style, telling people what they should do. He taught by example, modeling the principles of the kingdom of God. His own life was the textbook from which he taught.

### 3. Investor in Human Resources

Jesus taught that people come first, and the building of people is the most important component of a successful enterprise in this world. While he influenced powerfully all the lives he came in contact with, he had twelve disciples whom he prepared to continue his mission on earth after he left.

One of them was not genuine, but he worked with him, giving him every chance to learn, grow, and become a better person. He gave Judas every opportunity to become a success until he fired himself. He knew Judas could not jeopardize his mission. He could either be a part of its success or be a failure.

Jesus did not live in fear of every opposition that came his way; he knew what was mission sensitive and did his best to help all his disciples within that context, respecting their freedom to choose whether to cooperate with him or not. The same principle is in force today—those who in their selfishness are fighting against God's plan will either surrender to him or be failures.

### 4. Patience

He had a strategic plan and he worked it; he was willing to give up short-term gains for long-term results. When asked questions he knew were intended to trap him, he found skillful ways to deal with them without showing annoyance or anxiety. He sidestepped attempts to involve him in nonproductive controversies.

## 5. He Had Standards

There were things he was not going to do no matter how challenging the situation or how much pressure he got from those close to him. On one occasion he and his disciples were traveling through Samaria on their way to Jerusalem. They had to find a place to sleep overnight, so he sent some of his disciples into a Samaritan village to secure lodging.

They returned with the bad news that the villagers were not willing to host them. Two of the disciples, apparently angry at the rejection, asked if Jesus wanted them to call down fire from heaven and consume the village. Jesus rebuked them, and they went on to another village.

His disciples did not take into account the suffering they would create by burning the villagers and the mourning and grief that it would produce for their relatives. Anger makes us blind to the pain of others, and Jesus would have none of it.

## 6. Servant Leader

Robert Greenleaf is known as the modern father of servant leadership, a concept that developed in him while working for AT&T (American Telephone and Telegraph Company), as he became increasingly discontented with the authoritarian, power-centered leadership systems that existed in the United States during his time. He had deep concerns with the moral and ethical issues associated with that style.

In progressive organizations in today's world, the term leadership has replaced the term management, and the authoritarian style has been replaced by a participatory, collaborative style that is far more respectful and productive in harnessing the talent pool at a leader's disposal.

Servant leadership did not start with Robert Greenleaf—it started with Jesus, and he is its best model. He epitomizes the characteristics of empathy and compassion. In the training of his disciples, we see him empowering them to be the best they can be.

On one occasion Jesus and his disciples gathered in the house of a friend for a special supper. It was the custom of the time that the lowest ranked person washed the feet of the guests gathered for the meal. In a typical household, washing the feet of the guests would be the role of a servant or the youngest child mature enough to do it. For this gathering there were no servants, and none of the disciples wanted to be seen as less than the rest.

Jesus got up from supper, secured the necessary supplies, and washed his disciples' feet. When he was through, he told them, "Now that I, your Lord and Teacher, have washed your feet, you also should wash one another's feet. I have set you an example that you should do as I have done for you." (John 13:14, 15 NIV.)

## 7. Decisive and Forceful When Necessary

The temple at Jerusalem was the center of religious life for the Jewish people in Jesus's day. Especially at times of special celebrations, Jews and proselytes (non-Jew adherents to the Jewish faith) made pilgrimages from surrounding nations to worship at the Jerusalem temple.

The temple was the symbol of God's presence with his people and as such was to be treated with the reverence and respect due to a place of meeting with a holy god. In the interest of profiteering, the temple courts were being used for the sale of animals needed for sacrificial offerings and the exchange of money into temple currency for the purchase of the animals.

Jesus, on one of his visits to the temple, on seeing this unsightly spectacle, made a whip and chased the sellers, money changers, and animals out of the temple, restoring its due dignity and respect.

All leaders have to show initiative and drive if they are mission focused. Those who are content with only risk-free activity and waiting until all are behind them before they move will miss precious opportunities to make a difference in the world.

# THE PATH FORWARD

In the march of history, we see the guiding hand of our sovereign God in the affairs of our world while he allows us to make our mistakes and sometimes pay the price for them. In love and mercy, he is constantly pushing us toward being more loving and just in our dealings with each other.

It is easy to focus on the negatives—the wars, catastrophes natural and manmade, injustice, and unkindness—and not look at the positive things that are taking place in our world and especially in this country.

Efforts for the creation of a more just society have made significant strides in the past century. There is no question that we still have work to do—old practices are hard to change in some countries, and new infringements surface continually.

Today in many countries, we have the freedom to march in peaceful protest, a right we should not neglect to make use of when the circumstances warrant it. Failing to do so may allow the coming of a day when our rights are taken from us, and if we then ventured to march, it would be at the peril of our lives.

Now is not a time to lose hope and give in to those who would make us afraid. God is on the side of those who love truth. Evil will achieve temporary gains if we fail to stand for truth and righteousness. Ultimately God wins, and those who stand on his side will win with him.

President Trump is uniquely positioned to accomplish some things that few other presidents have had the opportunity to accomplish. He came to office without the overwhelming support of the party establishment and should not be beholden to them. He has not been part of the inner circle of the Washington establishment and therefore is not mentally bound by the cultural norms that exist there.

There are great expectations among those who supported him for the presidency that he will bring positive change to Washington as he promised (drain the swamp). He will receive even more support from the public if he makes the right moves to reform the self-serving systems of the Washington establishment and move to create a government that works for the people.

Recognizing his lack of experience in government, he needs to surround himself with competent, experienced people who can supply what he lacks. No one person knows everything, so a good team makes a tremendous difference in the world of leadership.

As he takes over the leadership of the nation, he cannot afford to be bogged down with the smallness of parochialism that pits our citizens against each other and against people of other countries or other religious or ethnic groups. The greatness of America is bigger than that.

Success will not come from following *The Art of the Deal* but from learning the art of dealing righteously with people according to the principles of the kingdom of God, which can be summed up in the words "Love your neighbor as yourself." (Mark 12:31 NIV.) If he walks down this path, he will find himself in harmony with God and will receive his blessings.

The approach of "divide and conquer" creates too many losers and moves society in the direction of the dark ages. The path forward is not one of intolerance, injustice, hate, and fear but of embracing the love and respect that unite and make winners of all who want to participate in the positive.

There is a wave of moral urgency moving across our world fueled by the energy of God himself. We see it in the end of slavery in the Americas, the victory of the Allied forces in the Second World War, the end of British colonial rule in India and the rest of the world, the successes of the civil-rights movement in the United States, the softening of atheistic communist systems, the end of apartheid in South Africa, and the creation of a more just society than we had fifty years ago.

A divine energy has been ignited in the hearts of people of conscience who, in love for humanity, get engaged in causes greater than themselves. Those who would seek to reverse this forward thrust stand in the way of God. In the end they will be moved out of the way like mud scraped from the farmer's shoes after he has walked in the field on a rainy day. They must remember that Napoleon had his Waterloo, Hitler his D-day, and Nixon his Watergate.

The nationalistic, isolationist rhetoric that is rising in the United States these days will take us backward rather than forward. Bridges always do better for people than walls. Bridges say both sides are prepared to live together in harmony and peace, enhancing each other's growth and development. Walls may seem to separate us from the evil others can do to us, but more significantly they prevent the flow of goodness between peoples, and that is the way of losers.

Mexico is our neighbor and should be treated with the kindness and respect of which Jesus spoke. Those given to hate may think they are doing this country a favor by being against Mexico and Mexicans, but any damage done to Mexico affects the United States.

When we create such economic hardship for the Mexican people, more of them will be finding their way across the border. If their health-care system fails because they do not have the money to maintain it, and communicable diseases spread, they will be coming across the border to us.

The United States was not immune to the danger of the Ebola outbreak in three African countries on the other side of the Atlantic. There was almost widespread panic when the first few cases were reported here. Scientists and health-care professionals from around the world worked feverishly to contain the spread of the virus—many at risk of their own lives.

We must wake up and face the facts that we live in a global village, and no man or nation is an island cut off from the rest of the world. Only by working together we can build a better future for ourselves and the rest of the world.

We must unite in praying for President Trump and his team, that they will plot a course for the country founded on love and mutual respect, that they will strive to preserve and improve old alliances with nations and industries that have served us well in the past, and that they will create new relationships that will help build a better future.

If he fails to execute his obligations for the people, it is the responsibility of Congress to hold him accountable and remove him if necessary.

If Congress fails to act, then it is the responsibility of the people to hold their congressional representatives accountable. If after dialogue they will not listen, then the people should launch a recall campaign and get them out of office, starting with the leadership.

Congress has already had its problems with low approval ratings for the past several years, gaining the reputation of being a "do-nothing Congress," so there is a lot of catching up for them to do on behalf of the American people.

With God, all things are possible. If the members of Congress will allow God to guide them, he can breathe new life into that organization just as he raised Lazarus from the dead.

The members of Congress need to look deep within and begin to focus on the American people whom they were placed there to serve. In failing to serve the people, they fail to serve God. To have responsibility for the well-being of other humans is a sacred trust for which God will hold them accountable.

Their responsibility is not to be purveyors of our hate and animosity toward political parties, persons, or policies we do not like but to constructively plot and execute a path forward for the nation that respects the rights of all its citizens and to deploy the nation's resources in a way that promotes the nation's peace and prosperity. They need to take leadership in elevating us to a higher level of integrity.

We as citizens have a responsibility in this also, and God will not always do for us what we should do for ourselves. We need to be more active in holding our elected officials accountable. We must do our parts to lift the standard of truth and integrity in our communities—doing what we can to eradicate divisiveness and creating a culture of tolerance and peace based on mutual respect.

Let us hope and pray that drastic action will not be necessary and that the nation will spend its energies creatively supporting its president on an agenda of respect and prosperity for all.

# CONCLUSION

The matter of greatest importance for each of us transcends who is president of the United States—it has to do with who we are as individuals and how we each relate to God, the source of our lives, without whom we would not exist. Are we honoring him with our lives by acknowledging his lordship and embracing the principles of his kingdom?

Have we found the purpose for which he has placed us in this world as ambassadors of his to show his love and goodness with the skills and talents he has given us within the sphere of influence opened to us? It is easy for us to analyze and criticize others and even God but overlook our wrongdoings and lost opportunities.

It is not so easy to look into the heart of divine righteousness and before his all-seeing eyes see our sinfulness, surrender to the acceptance of his ownership of our lives, and accept his invitation of saving grace.

Herein lies the power of the Christian gospel: not to wield in the creation of fear of the crusaders' swords or to have people tremble in hopelessness at the thunder of the hellfire preacher's voice, but rather to come to the consciousness that in our sovereign god is a heart of love, and in his embrace we find acceptance as we are and the saving grace to transform us into whom he intended for us to be.

No life is more beautiful than the one that radiates the presence of God in the world; no life more purposeful, rich, and fulfilling than a life in service to his cause; and no hope more inspiring than the hope of eternity with him.

The future of humanity is influenced by the actions of political leaders, but ultimately our future is in the hands of our great and wonderful God. Because of that I have hope. The tide of human activity may rise and fall from country to country as the ebb and flow of human decisions affect economies, safety, security, and people's freedoms. Behind and before it all is a guiding hand that steers not only the affairs of nations but my life and yours individually.

His love and mercy have sustained and blessed the human race through centuries of growth and development. He is constantly reaching out to us with a heart warm with compassion and forgiveness, inviting us into a trusting relationship with him. He has always had and always will have a special hand in the lives of those who look to him for personal care and guidance.

It is those who work with and for God who are the true movers and shakers of this world. We touch lives in ways that protect innocence, build character, and provide righteous leadership for time and eternity.

God's great workers are not always found in kings' palaces or presidential suites—we meet them daily on the busy streets of life, sharing a kind word, helping some weak soul to lift his or her heavy burden, or cheering a sad person with a song from the heart. The soldiers of God are those moved by compassion to take the time to relieve human suffering and to act beyond the words "I love you."

The beauty of God is seen in the flowers and forests of our land but with far greater grandeur in the lives of people transformed by his love and grace to rise above lives of anger and hate to love and goodness, from a sense of unworthiness and low self-esteem to the mastery of accepting that life is not about what you have but about who you are as a unique, valuable child of God's creation placed in this world for a noble purpose.

Yes, we would want to see a competent, efficient democratic administration in every country in the world. But that is not the reality of the world we live in. This world is filled with the tension between love and hate, good and evil, right and wrong, and truth and falsehood.

In every earthly system, there comes a day of accounting. For some it takes the form of an audit, stockholders' meeting, or performance evaluation; for elected officials it is Election Day; and for dictatorial systems, revolution day. For God and the earth, it is called judgment day.

The hand of God has shown—written through the march of time—that evil will not triumph in the end.

# CONCLUSION

Greed, selfishness, and hatred destroy themselves, and love ultimately wins. He who created the universe and holds the fate of the world in his hands is a loving God, and love cannot bear separation.

As he has been with those who loved him in the past, he is with his children now, and one day he will put an end to the separation from him that brought pain and suffering to our world. On that day all of us will give an account to God for how we have related to our fellow humans with the time and opportunity he has given us.

For those who chose his path of loving service, he will say, "Come, my children; inherit the kingdom prepared for you." For those who chose themselves, it will be final separation from life and the privilege of living in the beauty and joy of the divine presence.

Yes, in the end love will win. Amen.

www.ingramcontent.com/pod-product-compliance
Lightning Source LLC
Chambersburg PA
CBHW072057290426
44110CB00014B/1718